57

more

of the best

chocolate chip cookies

in the world

ALSO BY THE AUTHORS

57 more

of the best

chocolate chip cookies

in the world

*The Recipes That Won the Second National
Chocolate Chip Cookies Contest*

honey & larry zisman

ST. MARTIN'S GRIFFIN ⚘ NEW YORK

Design by Songhee Kim

Library of Congress Cataloging-in-Publication Data

Zisman, Honey.
    57 more of the best chocolate chip cookies in the world : the recipes that won the Second National Chocolate Chip Cookies Contest / Honey and Larry Zisman.—1st St. Martin's Griffin ed.
        p.   cm.
    Includes index.
    ISBN 0-312-15044-X
    1. Chocolate chip cookies.   I. Zisman, Larry.   II. Title.
TX772.Z59   1997
641.8'654—dc20   96-32864
                                                               CIP

First St. Martin's Griffin Edition: January 1997
10 9 8 7 6 5 4 3 2 1

for

emily ann

who will always have

chocolate chip cookies in her pockets

contents

No better treat
    will pass your lips,

Than these great cookies
    with chocolate chips

an everlasting favorite

QUESTION: *What do the Energizer Bunny and chocolate chip cookies have in common?*

ANSWER: *They both keep going and going and going . . . and going some more.*

It has been sixty-five years since Ruth Wakefield, owner of the Toll House Inn in Whitman, Massachusetts, created the beloved chocolate chip cookies known everywhere today as Toll House cookies. It was fifteen years ago that we created our first chocolate chip cookie contest. From over 5,000 entries, we selected the forty-seven best recipes and published them in a book called *The 47 Best Chocolate Chip Cookies in the World.* Seven printings and 200,000 copies later, we felt it was time to see what was new in the world of the chocolate chip, and we launched a second contest: "Chocolate Chip Cookies Forever." The response was overwhelming. More than 6,500 recipes arrived in our mailbox, proving that chocolate chip cookies are still the world's #1 favorite cookie, and demonstrating that home bakers are becoming more and more creative in dressing up and embellishing the basic chocolate chip cookie.

Fruits and nuts, liqueurs and candies, frostings and fillings—all were used in delicious and innovative ways to make chocolate chip cookies better and better, and to make them disappear faster and faster after being baked.

Just as in our first contest, it was not easy picking the winning recipes from so many worthy entries. But we worked long and hard, finally selecting the fifty-seven best-of-the-best cookie recipes. Our assignment certainly was not easy, but it was great fun and for a good cause: so you and all the world's chocolate chip cookie lovers can treat yourselves to the very best cookies possible.

And, yes, we know that children throughout the world and their children and their children's children—on and on through future millennia—will still be enjoying chocolate chip cookies as they blithely travel down information highways and hop from planet to planet.

Chocolate chip cookies forever!

suggestions for baking better cookies

It is quite popular these days to have a "Ten Best" or "Top Ten" list for all sorts of people and things, so it is quite appropriate to have a similar list for making cookies. But since chocolate chip cookies are so important, actually, twice as important as everything else, we have a list of the "Top Twenty Best Suggestions for Baking (and Enjoying) Better Chocolate Chip Cookies."

1. As you mix or beat or stir the ingredients together, scrape down the sides of the bowl to ensure that all the ingredients are evenly distributed and thoroughly mixed.
2. The new insulated cookie sheets with built-in air holes are a great improvement over the regular flat cookie sheets and do a better job of keeping the cookies from burning while they are in the oven.
3. There is an easy solution to the conflict over chewy cookies versus crispy cookies. You can satisfy both factions in your family by simply varying the baking times. To get chewy cookies, bake for less time; for crispy cookies, bake for more time.
4. All ovens vary in the exact temperature they maintain, so it is a good idea to keep checking on the cookies as they bake, whether it is for chewy cookies with a shorter baking time or for crispy cookies with a longer baking time.
5. Recipes are not commandments chiseled in stone. They are written on paper as something to be looked at, thought about, and changed in any

way you desire. If you like raisins better than the walnuts in the recipe, put in raisins instead. A chopped date can become a piece of crushed peppermint candy. Whole wheat flour can be substituted for white flour. Lemon zest can replace orange zest. You are the one doing the baking and eating, so make any alterations you want. You have to please only yourself—and those who eat your cookies.

6. Afraid that when following a recipe you will forget to add one or two ingredients? Here is a foolproof way to make sure you add everything you should. Before starting, read through the recipe and measure out each ingredient. Place them, in the order they are supposed to be added, on your work counter in small bowls or, in the case of spices, on individual squares of wax paper. As you prepare the cookies, just add the appropriate measured ingredient in turn.

7. Although a double boiler is convenient, you do not need one to melt chocolate. You can use a large pan and a small pot. Just fill the large pan with water and heat almost to boiling. Put the chocolate—and any other ingredients to be melted—in the small pot and place the pot in the hot water in the pan.

8. Tired of getting up to get more cookies because they are so good you can't stop eating them? Why not make them bigger—maybe two or three times bigger than usual—and then you can enjoy all the cookie eating you want without having to make repeated trips back to the cookie jar. Remember that larger cookies will bake differently than smaller ones, and you might have to experiment with longer baking times at lower temperatures.

9. It is important to grease the cookie sheets adequately to make sure the baked cookies slide off easily after they are removed from the oven. The cooking oil sprays are perfect for greasing cookie sheets.

10. If you do not have the time or energy to spoon out, position, and bake the dozens and dozens of cookies called for in a particular recipe, consider putting the cookie dough in a baking pan and making bar cookies instead. Of course, it will be necessary to adjust the cooking time and to check repeatedly with a toothpick to see when baking is done.

11. An easy way to make your cookies special after you have baked them is to put two cookies together with a filling to make a sandwich cookie. Here are some suggested fillings to get you started:

- peanut butter and jelly
- fruit jams
- marshmallow creme
- marshmallow creme mixed with flaked coconut
- melted chocolate
- marzipan
- poppy seed filling
- prune butter or apple butter
- chopped dates or figs
- cake frosting
- ice cream or frozen yogurt

12. You can make any cookie more festive by sprinkling colored sugar on top just before baking. The cookies will twinkle when they come out of the oven.

13. An added treat to put in your cookies is any candy that you have around the house. Besides chopping up almost any kind of candy bar, consider M&M's, spearmint leaves, jelly beans, chocolate-covered cordials, malted-milk balls, and licorice sticks, to name just a few.

14. A great idea for a party, a celebration, or a special gift is to make a giant-sized cookie—sort of a cookie pizza pie—that you can decorate with any message you want. Your imagination is the only limit to the occasions and decorations for this crowd pleaser.

15. Baked cookies (completely cooled) can be frozen in just about any kind of airtight container, including plastic storage bags. It is best to let the cookies defrost while still in their sealed container so that they do not absorb outside moisture.

16. Just as you can refreeze cookies that have already been frozen and thawed, you can also freeze the cookie dough you have prepared but not yet baked. It is best to leave the uncooked batter in its sealed container as it defrosts to prevent extra moisture from being absorbed. Also, defrost the batter in the refrigerator, rather than on a countertop.

17. Since cookie baking is one of the easiest creative pursuits in the kitchen, it is the perfect choice to introduce young children to cooking and baking. Mixing the ingredients is easy; it does not matter too much if the ingredients are not measured with absolute precision; and,

for most recipes, there is no danger from hot liquids boiling on the stove top. Best of all, children will enjoy eating the cookies they have made, getting a feeling of real accomplishment.

18. Since almost everyone brings either a bottle of wine or a bunch of flowers when going to someone else's home for dinner, why not bring a batch of homemade cookies instead. Anything homemade is more thoughtful and appreciated than something picked up in a store. And the cookies are an extra—they do not have to be served with your host's meal. Your host and hostess can enjoy them later, while thinking about your thoughtfulness and good taste.

19. Do you want to give a special gift that keeps on giving? Give someone a "Homemade Cookie of the Month" present, baking and sending them a different kind of cookie each month. Each cookie could be tied to a holiday or seasonal event during the month it is received.

20. Why not have a cookie-baking party for a young child's birthday or for a rainy-day activity? Several basic batters with varying ingredients and flavorings could be prepared, enough to make a dozen cookies for each child participating. Have dishes with different kinds of chopped fruits, chopped nuts, and pieces of candies so that each person can customize his or her own cookies. Everyone will have a good time tasting each other's creations.

This is our list of the top twenty best suggestions for baking and enjoying better chocolate chip cookies. Do you have more that you can add for yourself?

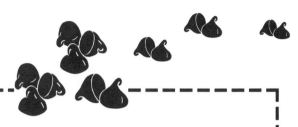

some

special

cookie

recipes

original nestlé® toll house® chocolate chip cookies

2¼ cups all-purpose flour
1 teaspoon baking soda
1 teaspoon salt
1 cup (2 sticks) butter, softened
¾ cup granulated sugar
¾ cup packed brown sugar
1 teaspoon vanilla extract

2 eggs
2 cups (12-ounce package)
  NESTLÉ TOLL HOUSE
  Semi-Sweet Chocolate
  Morsels
1 cup chopped nuts

Combine flour, baking soda, and salt in small bowl. Beat butter, granulated sugar, brown sugar, and vanilla in large mixer bowl. Add eggs one at a time, beating well after each addition; gradually beat in flour mixture. Stir in morsels and nuts. Drop by rounded tablespoon onto ungreased baking sheets.

Bake in preheated 375°F oven for 9 to 11 minutes, or until golden brown. Let stand for 2 minutes; remove to wire racks to cool completely.

yield: about 5 dozen cookies

PAN COOKIE VARIATION
Prepare dough as above. Spread into greased 15 × 10-inch jelly-roll pan. Bake in preheated 375°F oven for 20 to 25 minutes, or until golden brown. Cool in pan on wire rack. Makes about 4 dozen bars.

FOR HIGH-ALTITUDE BAKING (5,200 FEET)
Increase flour to 2½ cups. Add 2 teaspoons water with the flour and reduce both granulated sugar and brown sugar to ⅔ cup *each*. Bake at 375°F, drop cookies for 8 to 10 minutes and pan cookies for 17 to 19 minutes.

© Nestlé

A commercial for Nestlé Toll House Morsels has the jingle "I'm Bakin' Cookies" ("*Spending some time with you*"), based on the Fats Waller song "Ain't Misbehavin' " ("*Savin' all my love for you*").

hershey's "perfectly chocolate" chocolate chip cookies

2¼ cups all-purpose flour
⅓ cup HERSHEY'S Cocoa
1 teaspoon baking soda
½ teaspoon salt
1 cup (2 sticks) butter or
  margarine, softened
¾ cup granulated sugar

¾ cup packed light brown sugar
1 teaspoon vanilla extract
2 eggs
2 cups (12-ounce package)
  HERSHEY'S Semi-Sweet
  Chocolate Chips
1 cup chopped nuts (optional)

Heat oven to 375°F. Stir together flour, cocoa, baking soda, and salt. In large bowl, beat butter, granulated sugar, brown sugar, and vanilla on medium speed of electric mixer until creamy. Add eggs; beat well. Gradually add flour mixture, beating well. Stir in chocolate chips and nuts, if desired. Drop by rounded teaspoons onto ungreased cookie sheet. Bake 8 to 10 minutes, or until set. Cool slightly; remove from cookie sheet to wire rack.

yield: about 5 dozen cookies

PAN COOKIE VARIATION
Spread batter evenly in greased 15½ ×10½ ×1-inch jelly-roll pan. Bake at 375°F for 20 to 22 minutes, or until cookie begins to pull away from sides of pan. Cool completely in pan on wire rack. Cut into bars. Makes about 48 bars.

A trip to the city of Hershey, Pennsylvania, takes you to Hershey's Chocolate World, the official visitor's center of the famous chocolate maker, where you can make friends with costumed characters dressed as Reese's Peanut Butter Cups, Bar None candy bar, Hershey's Syrup, Hershey's Milk Chocolate bar, and Hershey's Symphony candy bar.

If you go during the three-day Presidents' Day weekend in February, you can participate in The Hotel Hershey's Chocolate Lovers Weekend. Delicious activities for this event include workshops where you can learn how to make various chocolate creations, tasting sessions for a variety of chocolate delights made by local chefs, special games for children, and scheduled tours of the town. As an added treat, you can also stroll down Cocoa Avenue and Chocolate Avenue, Hershey's two most favorite streets.

Chocolate lovers throughout the world owe a debt of gratitude to Steve Bailey of Lebanon, Pennsylvania.

Mr. Bailey has the important task of ensuring that the Hershey's Kisses that we buy are exactly the right size and the perfect shape—the curl on top has to be just so. He is a member of Hershey's manufacturing team and his job is to inspect the Kisses as they travel in front of him—at the rate of 20,000 a minute—along a conveyor belt from production to packaging. Mr. Bailey does not eat the defective Kisses he picks off the belt. The less-than-perfect chocolates are sent to the catch-off pan and then go back to the Rework Department to be melted down for another chance at perfection.

blue-ribbon chocolate chip cookies

DEBBI FIELDS   MRS. FIELDS COOKIES

2½ cups flour
½ teaspoon baking soda
¼ teaspoon salt
1 cup dark brown sugar
½ cup sugar

1 cup butter, softened
2 large eggs
2 teaspoons pure vanilla extract
2 cups semi-sweet chocolate
   chips

Preheat oven to 300°F.

In a medium-size bowl, combine flour, baking soda, and salt. Mix well with wire whisk. Set aside.

Using an electric mixer on medium speed, in a large bowl blend together brown sugar and sugar. Add butter and mix, scraping down sides of bowl, until a grainy paste is formed. Add eggs and vanilla, mixing at medium speed until light and fluffy. Add flour mixture and chocolate chips and blend at low speed until well mixed. Do not overmix.

Drop by rounded tablespoonfuls 2 inches apart onto ungreased cookie sheets. Cookies will spread quite a bit as they bake. Bake for 22 to 24 minutes, or until golden brown. Remove from oven and transfer cookies immediately with a spatula to a cool surface.

yield: approximately 3½ dozen cookies

Debbi Sivyer was thirteen years old back in 1971 when her sister was secretary to Charles O. Finley, the flamboyant owner of the Oakland Athletics baseball team in the American League. Debbi and her friend, fourteen-year-old Sheryl Lawrence, broke the gender barrier when Mr. Finley hired them to be the first ball girls in major league baseball.

Ms. Sivyer did more than just field foul balls in her white shorts, gold knee socks, and kelly-green jersey. She also served lemonade and chocolate chip cookies to the umpires between innings. This between-inning activity was an excellent experience for her when she eventually left baseball, got married, and founded Mrs. Fields Cookies.

kitchen-sink cookies

INNKEEPERS JIM AND BARBARA McLEAN

APPLES BED & BREAKFAST INN   BIG BEAR LAKE, CALIFORNIA

2½ cups old-fashioned oats
2 cups all-purpose flour
1 teaspoon baking powder
1 teaspoon baking soda
1 teaspoon salt
1 cup margarine
1 cup sugar
1 cup light brown sugar

½ cup creamy peanut butter
2 large eggs
2 teaspoons pure vanilla extract
2 cups semi-sweet chocolate chips
1½ cups chopped walnuts
1 cup flaked coconut
1 cup raisins

Preheat oven to 350°F.

Place oats in a food processor and pulse until oats are finely ground. Add flour, baking powder, baking soda, and salt and blend well. Set aside.

In a mixer, blend margarine and sugars until creamy. Add peanut butter, eggs, and vanilla and mix well. Add flour and oat mixture and mix until well incorporated, then add remaining ingredients and mix well.

Drop by rounded tablespoons onto cookie sheets sprayed with nonstick coating. Bake for 10 to 13 minutes, until light golden brown. Let cool on cookie sheets so cookies will have a crispy bottom.

yield: approximately 8 dozen cookies

In an article titled "A Winter Guide for Parents" in the "Weekend" section of The New York Times, Jan Benzel gives ideas for where to go and what to do to entertain your children in the big city. Her suggestions include museums, theaters that put on shows for children, and indoor playgrounds. Ms. Benzel insists that you should never go out without some snacks. She carries special surprises, kept secret until needed in real emergencies—for example, when your child starts crying in a taxi cab. And what is her particular recommendation for such emergencies? Chocolate! She also suggests that you carry baby wipes to clean up after the chocolate.

chocolate chip indulgence

PENNY'S PASTRIES   AUSTIN, TEXAS

¾ cup butter
4½ tablespoons shortening
¾ cup sugar
1½ cups firmly packed brown
    sugar
4½ cups unbleached flour
1½ teaspoons baking soda
1 teaspoon salt

2 tablespoons vanilla extract
3 large eggs
1½ tablespoons heavy cream or
    whole milk
¼ cup dark corn syrup
3 cups chocolate chips
1 cup broken pecans

Preheat oven to 350°F.

Cream together the butter, shortening, sugar, and brown sugar. Set aside.

Combine flour, baking soda, and salt. Set aside.

Mix together the vanilla, eggs, heavy cream, and corn syrup. Add butter mixture. Add flour mixture. Mix in chocolate chips and pecans.

Drop by heaping tablespoonfuls several inches apart onto greased cookie sheets. Bake for 15 minutes.

yield: approximately 3 dozen cookies

Are you looking for a memorable gift to give for a birthday or an anniversary? Is there a special occasion coming up that calls for proper acknowledgment? Do you want to show someone that you really love them? Why not send a bouquet of chocolate chip cookies from a company called, appropriately, Cookie Bouquets?

Cookie Bouquets—whose motto is "the edible alternative"—offers a dozen chocolate chip cookies wrapped and decorated in the style of an attractive flower arrangement that will surely tell anyone that you think they deserve something extra special. It's easy to contact Cookie Bouquets. Their toll-free number is 1-800-233-2171 or, in this high-tech era, you can reach them in cyberspace through the Internet at http://www.cookiebouquets.com.

chocolate chip cookies

EXECUTIVE CHEF PAUL ADAMO
HYATT REGENCY PRINCETON   PRINCETON, NEW JERSEY

⅞ cup sweet butter
1 cup margarine
1½ cups brown sugar
1½ cups sugar
4 or 5 eggs

2 teaspoons vanilla extract
1½ teaspoons baking soda
5¾ cups all-purpose flour
2 cups chocolate chips

Cream together the butter, margarine, brown sugar, and sugar until smooth. Add eggs slowly. Scrape the bowl thoroughly. Add vanilla and then add baking soda. Add flour all at once and mix only to incorporate. Add chocolate chips last. Refrigerate until dough is set.

Drop by tablespoonfuls 2 inches apart on greased cookie sheets. Bake at 350°F for 8 to 10 minutes.

yield: 4 to 5 dozen cookies

Besides getting a good feeling from doing a community service and helping others when you donate blood, there is the added reward of having all the doughnuts you want. Even better, though, after giving blood at the Red Cross donor drive at the Hyatt Regency Hotel in Princeton, New Jersey, we were given these great chocolate chip cookies.

They are definitely worth bleeding for!

The New York Philharmonic Orchestra gave a free concert in Central Park to a crowd of close to 100,000 music lovers. Even though this concert was free of charge to everyone, the orchestra did not neglect its most generous supporters. One hundred of these blue-chip contributors were entertained at a pre-concert reception where they munched on sun-dried tomato finger sandwiches and chocolate chip cookies.

peanut butter cookies with ghirardelli classic white chips

1 cup (2 sticks) butter at room
   temperature
½ cup sugar
1¼ cups brown sugar, packed
3 large eggs, at room
   temperature
1 cup chunky peanut butter

1 tablespoon vanilla extract
3 cups all-purpose flour
1 teaspoon baking soda
1 teaspoon salt
1 bag GHIRARDELLI
   CLASSIC WHITE CHIPS

In bowl of an electric mixer, beat butter and sugars on medium-high speed until creamy. Turn mixer down to lowest speed and add eggs one at a time, mixing well before adding the next egg. Add peanut butter and vanilla. Fold the flour, baking soda, and salt into the butter mixture. Fold in white chips. Stir until ingredients are well blended.

Preheat oven to 375°F. Roll 2 tablespoonfuls of cookie dough into a ball and place 2 inches apart on baking sheet. Dip a fork into a glass of cold water and make a criss-cross pattern, gently pressing dough down. Bake for 13 to 15 minutes. Store in airtight container at room temperature or in freezer for longer storage.

yield: about 4 dozen cookies

1 cup white chips = 6 ounces   1 11-ounce bag = 1¾ cups (approximately)

*Used with permission of the Ghirardelli Chocolate Company.

the prizewinning recipes from the second national chocolate chip cookies contest

ginger chews

STANLEY WOLFE　　　　CHERRY HILL, NEW JERSEY

1 cup flour
1 teaspoon baking soda
¼ teaspoon ground nutmeg
Dash of salt
½ cup shortening
¾ cup packed brown sugar

1 egg
1 teaspoon vanilla extract
½ cup finely chopped candied
　ginger
½ cup chopped walnuts
1 cup chocolate chips

Preheat oven to 375°F.

Sift together the flour, baking soda, nutmeg, and salt. Set aside.

Cream together the shortening and brown sugar. Add egg and vanilla. Stir in flour mixture, candied ginger, walnuts, and chocolate chips.

Drop by teaspoonfuls onto greased cookie sheets. Bake for 10 to 12 minutes.

yield: approximately 4 dozen cookies

The usual weapons of war are destructive bullets, bombs, and artillery. But there is another weapon of war, even more powerful than exploding ordnance: chocolate.

In a "My Turn" column in Newsweek magazine, journalist and novelist Herbert Mitgang relates how American soldiers in the NATO peacekeeping force in Bosnia are winning over the local populace just as he saw happen in Europe during and after World War II: giving out food—especially chocolate bars—to the people.

cran-brandy squares

NORMA LEHMAN   WEST DES MOINES, IOWA

1½ cups uncooked quick rolled
    oats
14 ounces sweetened condensed
    milk
1 tablespoon fruit-flavored
    brandy

¼ teaspoon salt
½ cup dried cranberries
2¼ cups chocolate chips

Preheat oven to 350°F.

Stir together the oats, condensed milk, fruit-flavored brandy, salt, cranberries, and chocolate chips until thoroughly mixed.

Scrape batter into a greased 8-inch-square baking pan. Pat down evenly with dampened hands. Bake for 25 to 30 minutes. Remove from oven and let cool. Cut into 1½-inch squares.

yield: approximately 2 dozen cookies

Laboratory-created "environmental fragrances" are being used in retail stores to create a friendly atmosphere, in hotel lobbies to impart a natural-smelling freshness, and in certain hospitals (such as New York's Memorial-Sloan Kettering Cancer Center, which uses whiffs of sweet vanilla) to reduce stress among patients.

Even Disney World in Florida has joined this trend. Visitors to Epcot's Magic House, a model home with specific scents in each room, has in the kitchen the aroma of chocolate chip cookies baking.

angel wings

AMY BOSWELL　　　　TOWSON, MARYLAND

1 cup shortening
½ cup sugar
½ cup packed brown sugar
1 egg
1 teaspoon vanilla extract
3 cups corn flakes cereal
½ cup finely chopped pecans

¼ cup butterscotch chips
1 cup milk chocolate candy bar
　pieces
1 cup flaked coconut
60 cut-up pieces of glacé
　apricots or peaches

Preheat oven to 350°F.

Cream shortening, then add sugar and brown sugar, beating until light. Add egg and beat well. Stir in vanilla, corn flakes, pecans, butterscotch chips, and chocolate candy bar pieces. Drop by teaspoonfuls 2 inches apart onto greased cookie sheets.

Place a small mound of coconut in the center of each cookie, pressing down lightly. Put a piece of glacé fruit in center of coconut. Bake for 8 to 10 minutes. Carefully remove cookies from cookie sheets while still warm.

yield: 5 dozen cookies

triple treat perks

ADRIENNE FOLEY   IOWA CITY, IOWA

1 cup flour
1 teaspoon baking powder
¼ teaspoon salt
½ cup margarine or shortening
½ cup sugar
½ cup brown sugar

1 egg
1 teaspoon strong coffee
½ cup white chocolate chips
½ cup milk chocolate chips
½ cup semi-sweet chocolate chips
Mocha Filling (recipe follows)

Preheat oven to 375°F.

Sift together flour, baking powder, and salt. Set aside.

Cream together the margarine, sugar, and brown sugar. Mix in egg and coffee. Stir in flour mixture. Add white chocolate chips, milk chocolate chips, and semisweet chocolate chips. Drop by teaspoonfuls onto greased cookie sheets.

Bake for 10 to 12 minutes. Remove from oven and let cool. Spread Mocha Filling on top of half of the cookies and then cover filling with remaining cookies.

yield: approximately 2 dozen cookies

MOCHA FILLING

3 tablespoons margarine
¼ cup cocoa powder
1½ to 2 cups confectioners'
    sugar

¼ cup strong coffee

Mix together well the margarine, cocoa powder, confectioners' sugar, and coffee until creamy.

In an advertising campaign to increase the consumption of milk, the California Milk Processor Board launched a $22 million promotion effort. The campaign was a series of humorous advertisements showing the horrors of having a desired food but no milk to drink with it. And what was the highly desired food that was left milkless? Chocolate chip cookies, of course.

hazelnut kisses

ANNE DEMPSEY   PARMA, OHIO

1½ cups chopped hazelnuts
½ cup butter, softened
1 egg
2 teaspoons vanilla extract
½ cup sugar

½ cup packed brown sugar
1½ cups flour
1 teaspoon baking soda
½ cup mini chocolate chips
36 chocolate Kisses

Preheat oven to 350°F.

Place hazelnuts in a single layer in a shallow pan and bake for 6 to 8 minutes, stirring once or twice, until lightly toasted. Remove from oven and set aside.

Mix together the butter, egg, vanilla, sugar, brown sugar, flour, and baking soda. Stir in toasted hazelnuts and chocolate chips.

Using slightly dampened hands, encase each chocolate Kiss in a 1-inch ball of batter. Place cookies on greased cookie sheets. Bake for 11 to 13 minutes.

yield: 3 dozen cookies

Teuscher chocolates are flown in twice every week from Switzerland, where they are made, to their Fifth Avenue store in Manhattan.

A not-to-be-missed spot on Upper Hatch Street in Dublin, Ireland, is the Chocolate Bar, an elegant saloon that serves trademark shots of chocolate vodka. Condé Nast Traveler magazine describes the elegant interior decor of the Chocolate Bar—with its green sofas, gilt mirrors, and lush velvet curtains covering stone walls—as "rich as caramel, dark as bittersweet, and sinfully smooth as a cream-filled center." The Chocolate Bar, we are told, is every bit as addictive as its name.

gil's greatest

GILBERT WYATT   NEWPORT NEWS, VIRGINIA

2 cups flour
1 teaspoon baking powder
¾ cup shortening
1 cup confectioners' sugar
1 egg
2 ounces semi-sweet chocolate,
   melted

1 teaspoon vanilla extract
¼ cup sour cream
½ cup semi-sweet mini chocolate
   chips
Coffee Frosting (recipe
   follows)

Preheat oven to 350°F.

Sift together the flour and baking powder. Set aside.

Cream together the shortening and sugar. Add egg and melted chocolate, mixing together well. Stir in vanilla, sour cream, and chocolate chips.

Drop by teaspoonfuls onto greased cookie sheets. Bake for 11 to 13 minutes. Remove from oven and let cool. Top cookies with Coffee Frosting.

yield: approximately 4 dozen cookies

COFFEE FROSTING

2 cups confectioners' sugar

¼ cup very strong coffee

2 teaspoons margarine, softened

Mix together well confectioners' sugar, margarine, and coffee, until creamy.

The motto of the Norm Thompson catalog company based in Portland, Oregon, is "Escape from the Ordinary," and the company lives up to it when it comes to chocolate. Items in the catalog include

- *Noah's Ark in milk chocolate with pairs of elephants, squirrels, bears, and monkeys made out of milk and dark chocolate*
- *a milk-chocolate dinosaur egg filled with milk-chocolate and bittersweet-chocolate baby dinosaurs*
- *mice made of Swiss chocolate, filled with creamy and crunchy hazelnut praline, and packed in a cardboard wedge that looks like a piece of Swiss cheese*

peppermint hats

BECKY NOVOTNY   ST. PAUL, MINNESOTA

1 cup finely chopped almonds
1 cup butter
1 cup sugar
1 egg, separated
2 cups flour

1 ounce unsweetened chocolate, melted
1 cup chocolate chips
25 chocolate-covered peppermint patties

Preheat oven to 350°F.

Place almonds in a single layer in a shallow pan and bake for 6 to 8 minutes, stirring once or twice, until lightly toasted. Remove from oven and set aside.

Lower oven temperature to 300°F.

Cream together the butter and sugar. Add egg yolk and mix together well. Stir in flour and melted chocolate. Stir in toasted almonds and chocolate chips.

Press batter into a greased and floured 8-inch-square pan. Brush egg white over top. Place chocolate-covered peppermint patties evenly in 5 rows of 5 over top of batter, pressing each one down slightly. Bake for 30 to 35 minutes. Remove from oven and let cool. Cut into 5 rows of 5 cookies, with each cookie having a peppermint patty top.

yield: 25 cookies

There is now an easy and unequivocal way to show off your passion for chocolate chip cookies, besides eating them every day. The Potpourri catalog from Medfield, Massachusetts, offers a 2-foot-high table lamp in the shape of a giant chocolate chip cookie. The lamp not only is UL-approved, but also comes with a 150-watt bulb giving enough light so that you can see every crumb sitting on your plate of cookies, ensuring that not a single morsel will be missed.

frosted hermits

BONNIE GRAY   BILOXI, MISSISSIPPI

1¾ cups flour
1 teaspoon baking powder
½ teaspoon baking soda
Dash of salt
1 teaspoon cinnamon
½ teaspoon ground nutmeg
Dash of ground cloves
½ cup margarine, softened

1 cup packed brown sugar
1 egg
½ cup sour cream
½ cup raisins
1 cup chopped pecans
1½ cups mini chocolate chips
Cream Cheese Frosting (recipe
    follows)

Preheat oven to 325°F.

Sift together the flour, baking powder, baking soda, salt, cinnamon, nutmeg, and cloves. Set aside.

Beat together the margarine, brown sugar, and egg. Stir in sour cream and mix well. Slowly stir in flour mixture. Add raisins, pecans, and chocolate chips.

Drop by teaspoonfuls 2 inches apart onto greased cookie sheets. Bake for 13 to 15 minutes. Remove from oven and let cool. Top with Cream Cheese Frosting.

yield: approximately 4 dozen cookies

CREAM CHEESE FROSTING

3 ounces cream cheese
1 tablespoon milk

2 teaspoons coffee liqueur
2 cups confectioners' sugar

Mix together the cream cheese, milk, and coffee liqueur. Slowly stir in confectioners' sugar, mixing until completely smooth.

sunshiners

BRENDA EDELMAN   MIAMI, FLORIDA

1 cup margarine
1 cup packed brown sugar
2 eggs
2½ cups flour
1½ tablespoons milk
½ teaspoon baking soda

1 tablespoon ginger liqueur
1 cup orange marmalade
1 cup chopped candied fruit
1 cup chopped candied cherries
1 cup chopped pecans
1 cup chocolate chips

Preheat oven to 325°F.

Cream together the margarine and sugar. Add eggs, flour, milk, baking soda, ginger liqueur, and orange marmalade. Mix in candied fruits, candied cherries, pecans, and chocolate chips.

Drop by teaspoonfuls onto greased cookie sheets. Bake for 16 to 18 minutes.

yield: approximately 8 dozen cookies

Maison du Chocolat, the French chocolate maker headquartered in Paris, has a new drink called La Tasse de Chocolat, which translates as "The Chocolate Cup." The drink comes in small milk bottles, about a pint, and contains a perfect mixture of chocolate, cocoa, low-fat milk, water, sugar, and vanilla. The label instructs you to heat the drink gently, and declares that each bottle holds two servings. But the smooth, rich delight can really be shared among three or four fortunate people. A bottle of La Tasse de Chocolat costs about $10 and is available at Maison du Chocolat shops in Paris, New York, and other major cities.

longhorn gems

CARLA FIELDS   HITCHCOCK, TEXAS

1 cup butter or margarine
1 cup sugar
½ cup brown sugar
2 eggs
2 cups flour

1 teaspoon baking soda
2 teaspoons chocolate mint
   liqueur
1 cup chopped walnuts
1½ cups mint chocolate chips

Preheat oven to 350°F.

Cream together the butter, sugar, and brown sugar. Add eggs, flour, and baking soda. Mix in chocolate mint liqueur, walnuts, and chocolate chips.

Drop by teaspoonfuls onto greased cookie sheets. Bake for 10 to 12 minutes. Remove from oven and let cool before removing from cookie sheets.

yield: approximately 6 dozen cookies

Sign posted in Zagara's, an upscale home furnishings and gourmet food store in Marlton, New Jersey, near Philadelphia:

> PLEASE KEEP CHILDREN IN HAND.
> UNATTENDED CHILDREN WILL BE DIPPED
> IN CHOCOLATE AND FED TO THE MANAGER.

grandma's orange creme sandwiches

ANITA MILLS   NEW BRITAIN, CONNECTICUT

2 cups flour
1 teaspoon baking soda
1 teaspoon baking powder
1 cup sugar
1 cup brown sugar
2 eggs
1 cup oil
Dash of salt

2 teaspoons black walnut extract
2 cups uncooked quick rolled
   oats
1 cup chopped walnuts
1 cup chocolate chunks
Orange Creme Filling (recipe
   follows)

Preheat oven to 350°F.

Sift together the flour, baking soda, and baking powder. Set aside.

Mix together the sugar, brown sugar, eggs, oil, salt, and black walnut extract. Stir in flour mixture, oats, walnuts, and chocolate chunks.

Using dampened hands, drop teaspoon-sized portions of batter onto greased cookie sheets. Bake for 13 to 15 minutes. Remove from oven and let cool. Spread Orange Creme Filling on half of the cookies and then cover filling with remaining half of the cookies.

yield: approximately 3 dozen cookies

ORANGE CREME FILLING

2 cups confectioners' sugar   *1 teaspoon orange extract*
4 to 5 tablespoons orange juice   *½ teaspoon orange zest*

Mix together the confectioners' sugar, orange juice, orange extract, and orange zest until creamy.

Maggie Lyon Chocolatiers of Norcross, Georgia, less than twenty miles from the 1996 Olympic Games in Atlanta, makes everyone a winner. The company has created a milk-chocolate medallion wrapped in gold foil displaying the official logo of the 1996 Atlanta Olympics. This "Olympic Medal" even comes with a red, white, and blue ribbon so you can wear it around your neck just like a true Olympic champion. The company is named after the founder's grandmother, Maggie Lyon, a pioneer woman from Ohio who operated a stagecoach stop until she retired at the age of ninety-two.

my mother's chocolate chip strudel bars

CATHY WADDELL   ABINGTON, PENNSYLVANIA

1½ cups chopped figs
1 cup water
1½ cups sugar
2 tablespoons cornstarch
2 tablespoons lemon juice
3 teaspoons lemon zest
2½ cups flour

½ teaspoon baking powder
¼ teaspoon salt
1 cup butter
½ cup chopped dates
½ cup chopped dried apricots
1 cup chocolate chips

Place figs and water in a heavy saucepan, heat to boiling, and continue cooking for about 7 minutes, until figs are soft and water is nearly gone. Remove from heat.

Stir in ½ cup of the sugar, the cornstarch, 1½ tablespoons of the lemon juice, and 2 teaspoons of the lemon zest. Set aside.

Preheat oven to 350°F.

Sift together the flour, baking powder, and salt. Set aside.

Cream together the butter and remaining 1 cup sugar. Mix in remaining ½ tablespoon of the lemon juice, remaining 1 teaspoon of the lemon zest, the dates, and apricots. Stir in flour mixture and chocolate chips.

Press approximately three quarters of the batter into a greased 9 × 13-inch pan. Spread fig mixture evenly over top of batter in pan. Sprinkle remaining quarter of the batter over fig mixture. Bake for 30 to 35 minutes. Remove from oven and let cool. Cut into 2-inch squares.

yield: approximately 3 dozen cookies

When Debbi Fields, the guiding force behind Mrs. Fields cookies, proposed starting her now very successful chain of cookie shops, she was told by the experts: "A cookie store is a bad idea. Besides, the market research report shows that America likes crispy cookies, not soft and chewy like you make."

Did the Wright brothers also receive the advice that man can never fly?

lemon bowls

CHARLES BECKER   PASADENA, CALIFORNIA

¾ cup butter, softened
½ cup sugar
1½ cups flour
2 teaspoons lemon zest
1 egg yolk

1 cup mini chocolate chips
1 egg white, beaten slightly
½ cup finely ground almonds
Lemon Icing (recipe follows)

Preheat oven to 375°F.

Cream together the butter and sugar. Beat in flour, lemon zest, egg yolk, and chocolate chips. Form dough into 1-inch balls and coat with egg white. Roll the balls in ground almonds and place on greased cookie sheets.

Press your thumb into the center of each ball, forming a small bowl. Bake for 12 to 15 minutes. Remove from oven and let cool. Spoon Lemon Icing into thumbprint bowl.

yield: approximately 2½ dozen cookies

LEMON ICING

1 cup confectioners' sugar
Zest of ½ lemon

2 tablespoons lemon juice

Mix together well the confectioners' sugar, lemon zest, and lemon juice.

He may have flown in the opposite direction, but he sure knew what to take to eat when he went.

Douglas "Wrong Way" Corrigan became an instant American folk hero in July 1938 when he left Floyd Bennett Field in Brooklyn and flew his airplane to Dublin, Ireland. What made his trip so very noteworthy, getting all the public attention, was that he had filed a flight plan to go from New York to Long Beach, California, but, instead, wound up on the other side of the Atlantic Ocean.

Mr. Corrigan, with tongue firmly in cheek, said that somehow he had made a wrong turn and had not realized that he was going eastward over the ocean toward Europe rather than westward across the United States to California. His explanation, however, seemed a little far-fetched to United States aviation authorities. They had denied him permission to fly across to Europe because they deemed his airplane unfit to make the trans-Atlantic flight.

Whatever his sense of direction, "Wrong Way" had the right stuff when it came to his nourishment. He took with him two boxes of fig crackers, a quart of water, and a few chocolate bars.

zowies

CHARLENE SHEPPARD   NEW BRUNSWICK, NEW JERSEY

½ cup margarine
1¼ cups sugar
1 cup graham cracker crumbs
1 cup crushed peanut brittle
   candy
½ cup flour
½ teaspoon baking powder
¼ teaspoon salt

1 egg
2 tablespoons milk
½ teaspoon vanilla extract
½ teaspoon almond extract
½ cup flaked coconut
¾ cup chocolate chips
Confectioners' sugar

Preheat oven to 350°F.

Mix together the margarine, ¼ cup of the sugar, graham cracker crumbs, and peanut brittle. Pat batter into a greased 9 × 13-inch pan. Bake for 10 minutes. Remove from oven and set aside.

Sift together the flour, baking powder, and salt. Set aside.

Beat egg until light. Add remaining 1 cup of sugar, beating well. Add flour mixture, milk, vanilla, almond extract, coconut, and chocolate chips.

Spread evenly over baked batter in pan. Bake for 25 to 30 minutes, until light brown. Remove from oven and let cool. Sprinkle confectioners' sugar over top. Cut into 2-inch squares.

yield: approximately 3 dozen cookies

While chocolate means happiness and enjoyment to most people, chocolate was partly responsible for a government crisis in Sweden in 1995, preventing the deputy prime minister from being elevated to prime minister.

Deputy Prime Minister Mona Sahlin was a popular, energetic, and attractive public official and the designated successor to Prime Minister Invar Carlsson, who was going to retire. Unfortunately, Ms. Sahlin had used an official Swedish government credit card to buy some personal items. While the Swedish people are quite tolerant of sexual activities that would doom a politician in other countries, they are extraordinarily strict and unforgiving when it comes to financial irregularities, no matter how trivial. Ms. Sahlin paid the credit card bills herself but the damage had been done.

And what had she purchased?

Diapers and chocolate bars.

jelly bean gee-willikers

CHRISTINA EGAN   WALTHAM, MASSACHUSETTS

2 cups flour
1 teaspoon baking soda
½ teaspoon salt
1 cup shortening
1½ cups sugar

2 eggs
1 teaspoon vanilla extract
1 cup mini jelly beans, a variety
   of flavors
1 cup chocolate chips

Preheat oven to 375°F.

Sift together the flour, baking soda, and salt. Set aside.

Beat shortening with the sugar. Mix in eggs, vanilla, and flour mixture. Stir in jelly beans and chocolate chips.

Drop by tablespoonfuls 2 inches apart onto greased cookie sheets. Place cookie sheets, one at a time, on middle shelf in oven and bake for 13 to 15 minutes.

yield: approximately 5½ dozen cookies

Are you looking for a unique way to serve hot cocoa?

Try this: use a heavy silver-plated nickel English Army chocolate pitcher from the 1950s. These old silver service items were gathered from British Army mess halls throughout the Empire—from Aden to Zanzibar—and are available from the J. Peterman Company, the whimsical but endlessly romantic catalog dispatched from Lexington, Kentucky.

zesty honey bars

CHERYL FORD   BOISE, IDAHO

1 cup flour
1 teaspoon baking powder
Dash of salt
3 eggs, beaten
1 cup honey

Zest of 1 lemon
1 cup chopped dates
1 cup chopped pecans
1 cup chocolate chips
Confectioners' sugar

Preheat oven to 325°F.

Sift together the flour, baking powder, and salt. Set aside.

Beat together the eggs, honey, and lemon zest. Stir in flour mixture. Add dates, pecans, and chocolate chips.

Pour batter into a greased 9 × 13-inch pan. Bake for 45 to 50 minutes. Remove from oven and let cool. Sprinkle confectioners' sugar over top. Cut into 2-inch squares.

yield: approximately 3 dozen cookies

The "Bistro" cart in Newark International Airport held carry-on lunch-boxes for Continental Airlines passengers to pick up and take with them as they boarded their flights. The lunches contained everything a traveler could want: a ham and cheese sandwich on a roll; a bag of taco chips; a container of spring water; and, for dessert, some chocolate chip cookies.

peanut butter gems

CINDY DENNIS   SILVER SPRING, MARYLAND

1 cup flour	½ cup sugar
¼ teaspoon baking soda	½ cup brown sugar
¼ teaspoon baking powder	1 egg
¼ teaspoon salt	½ teaspoon maple flavoring
½ cup shortening	½ cup M&M's Mini Baking Bits
½ cup peanut butter	½ cup chocolate chips

Preheat oven to 400°F.

Sift together the flour, baking soda, baking powder, and salt. Set aside.

Cream together the shortening, peanut butter, sugar, and brown sugar. Mix in egg and maple flavoring. Stir in flour mixture. Add M&M's Mini Baking Bits and chocolate chips.

Roll into 1-inch balls and place on greased cookie sheets. Bake for 9 to 11 minutes.

yield: approximately 4 dozen cookies

The Blackhawk Waterways Convention and Visitors Bureau in Illinois offers free for the asking "The Blackhawk Chocolate Trail Guide."

This information packet is a great guide for tourists who want to visit the many businesses offering chocolate specialties in four counties (Carroll, Whiteside, Lee, and Ogle) in northwestern Illinois. You can obtain "The Blackhawk Chocolate Trail Guide" by calling (800) 678-2108.

dad's favorite

CLAUDIA ROBINSON   ROTTERDAM, NEW YORK

1 cup flour
½ teaspoon baking soda
¼ teaspoon salt
½ cup butter or margarine
½ cup sugar
¼ cup packed brown sugar

1 egg
1 teaspoon vanilla extract
2 tablespoons honey
½ cup uncooked quick rolled oats
1 cup chocolate chips
½ cup chopped almonds

Preheat oven to 375°F.

Sift together the flour, baking soda, and salt. Set aside.

Beat together the butter, sugar, and brown sugar. Add in egg, vanilla, and honey. Stir in flour mixture. Add oats, chocolate chips, and almonds.

Drop by teaspoonfuls 2 inches apart onto greased cookie sheets. Bake for 9 to 11 minutes.

yield: approximately 4 dozen cookies

Chicago may be the city with broad shoulders, but if you go one hundred miles west to Oregon, Illinois, you will find a place for people with broad cravings for chocolate.

The Pinehill Bed and Breakfast on Mix Street in Oregon has just about everything for chocolate lovers. The inn, built in 1874 in the style of an Italian country villa, offers guests a smorgasbord of homemade fudge, cocoa, and expensive boxed chocolates from both this country and Europe. Guests find Hershey's Kisses and rose petals on their antique beds when they go to sleep at night.

Sharon Burdick, the owner of the inn after a career in marketing in Chicago, has a collection of books all about chocolate that guests can browse through. Ms. Burdick also has a mail-order fudge business with no fewer than thirty flavors, including all kinds of chocolate and nut combinations plus Pilgrim Fudge, which is made with sun-dried cranberries, orange spice, and walnuts.

You can make reservations or order fudge by calling the Pinehill Bed and Breakfast at (815) 732-2061. (No, the telephone number is not (800) I LOVE CHOCOLATE.)

sugar plums

DIANA HIGGINS   WASHINGTON, D.C.

¾ cup flour
½ teaspoon baking soda
Dash of salt
½ cup butter
1 cup sugar
1 egg
½ teaspoon vanilla extract

¼ teaspoon ground ginger
1½ cups uncooked quick rolled
   oats
1 cup chopped candied fruit
¾ cup chocolate chips
Sugar

Preheat oven to 350°F.

Sift together the flour, baking soda, and salt. Set aside.

Mix together the butter, 1 cup of sugar, egg, vanilla, and ginger. Stir in flour mixture, oats, candied fruit, and chocolate chips.

Shape batter into 1-inch balls and roll in sugar. Place cookies 2 inches apart on greased cookie sheets. Bake for 12 to 14 minutes.

yield: approximately 4 dozen cookies

cherry chips

ARTHUR POGUE   ARLINGTON, TEXAS

1 cup crushed chocolate
    sandwich cookies
¾ cup flour
½ teaspoon baking soda
½ teaspoon baking powder
½ cup margarine
2 ounces unsweetened chocolate
1 cup sugar
½ cup cottage cheese

1 egg, slightly beaten
1 teaspoon cherry-flavored
    brandy
½ teaspoon vanilla extract
1 cup chopped maraschino
    cherries
1 cup chocolate chips
½ cup chopped pecans

Preheat oven to 375°F.

Mix together the crushed cookies, flour, baking soda, and baking powder.
Set aside.

Place margarine and unsweetened chocolate in a heavy saucepan and heat,
stirring, until melted. Remove from heat and let cool slightly. Stir in sugar, cottage cheese, egg, cherry-flavored brandy, and vanilla. Stir in flour mixture. Add
cherries, chocolate chips, and pecans.

Drop by teaspoonfuls onto greased cookie sheets. Bake for 11 to 13 minutes.
Gently remove cookies from cookie sheets while still warm.

yield: approximately 4 dozen cookies

after-school gimmees

RHODA WILKINSON   BRIGHTON, COLORADO

¾ cup flour
1 teaspoon baking powder
Dash of salt
¾ cup cornmeal
¾ cup shortening
¾ cup sugar

1 egg
1 teaspoon vanilla extract
¾ cup raisins
1 cup chopped walnuts
1 cup chocolate chips

Preheat oven to 350°F.

Sift together the flour, baking powder, and salt. Mix in cornmeal. Set aside.

Mix together the shortening, sugar, egg, and vanilla. Stir in flour mixture. Add in raisins, walnuts, and chocolate chips.

Drop by teaspoonfuls onto greased cookie sheets. Bake for 13 to 15 minutes.

yield: approximately 5 dozen cookies

There are museums for just about everything, so it should be no surprise that there is a chocolate museum in Lititz, Pennsylvania, a few miles north of Lancaster in Pennsylvania Dutch country.

The Wilbur Chocolate Candy Americana Museum & Store is an adjunct to the factory of the Wilbur Chocolate Company. The museum has exhibits of antique candy-packaging equipment, cocoa tins, advertisements, candy-making tools, and a collection of chocolate pots—with names like Dresden and Limoges—dating to the 1700s. In addition, museum visitors can see candy being made the old-fashioned way—by hand.

All this is for free since there is no admission charge to the museum.

fruitychews

DORIS KRAUS   EVANSTON, ILLINOIS

1 cup margarine, softened
1 egg
2½ cups flour
2 cups confectioners' sugar
1 teaspoon baking soda
1 teaspoon cream of tartar

Dash of salt
2 teaspoons vanilla extract
1½ cups cut-up Aplets &
   Cotlets candies
1 cup chocolate chips

Preheat oven to 375°F.

Mix together the margarine, egg, flour, confectioners' sugar, baking soda, cream of tartar, salt, vanilla, Aplets & Cotlets candies, and chocolate chips.

Drop by teaspoonfuls 3 inches apart onto greased cookie sheets. Bake for 7 to 8 minutes. Remove from oven. Remove cookies from cookie sheets while slightly warm.

yield: approximately 6 dozen cookies

The Austrian capital city of Vienna is the scene of perhaps more formal balls than anywhere else, with more than three hundred affairs held each year, ranging from the most opulent and lavish Opera Ball to the comparatively more egalitarian Taxi Driver's Ball.

But of all of these sparkling gatherings, none is sweeter than the Bonbon Ball, sponsored by the Süsswarenhändler, the candy and sweet dealers of Austria. The highlight of the ball is the crowning of Miss Bonbon, a beauty contest in which the winner is given her weight in chocolate. A very lucky young lady, indeed.

peanut pearls

ALLYSON JACKSON   ATLANTA, GEORGIA

2 cups brown sugar
½ teaspoon salt
2 egg whites, beaten stiff

2 cups finely ground peanuts
1 cup milk-chocolate chips
1 cup semi-sweet chocolate chips

Preheat oven to 325°F.

Fold brown sugar and salt into egg whites. Fold in ground peanuts, milk-chocolate chips, and semi-sweet chocolate chips, stirring as little as possible.

Roll into tablespoon-sized balls and place onto greased cookie sheets. Bake for 14 to 15 minutes.

yield: approximately 4 dozen cookies

Health and nutrition writer Jane E. Brody suggests a variety of suitable snacks to take with you for your children when traveling. Among her suggestions are fruit juices, skim milk, fresh fruit, sandwiches of lean packaged cold cuts or lentil spread on whole-grain bread, low-fat cheese and yogurt, low-salt pretzels, and unbuttered popcorn.

However, Ms. Brody assures her readers that "You need not be a fanatic" and, since family vacation trips are not taken too often, "It would not undermine your child's health to have a couple of soft drinks or chocolate chip cookies while in transit."

oregon oats

GAIL TUTTLE   BEAVERTON, OREGON

1½ cups flour
1 teaspoon baking soda
¼ teaspoon salt
1 cup shortening
1 cup sugar
½ cup brown sugar
2 eggs

2 teaspoons vanilla extract
2 cups uncooked quick rolled
    oats
¾ cup chopped hazelnuts
¾ cup dried cranberries or raisins
¾ cup chocolate chips

Preheat oven to 350°F.

Sift together the flour, baking soda, and salt. Set aside.

Beat together the shortening, sugar, and brown sugar until fluffy. Add eggs and vanilla. Stir in flour mixture, oats, hazelnuts, cranberries, and chocolate chips.

Drop by teaspoonfuls onto greased cookie sheets. Bake for 10 to 12 minutes.

yield: approximately 6 dozen cookies

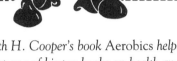

In 1968, Dr. Kenneth H. Cooper's book Aerobics helped launch the fitness movement. It is just one of his ten books on health and well-being, and has sold more than 10 million copies in the United States alone. Dr. Cooper oversees the Dallas-based Cooper Aerobics Center, which includes a clinic, a health club, hotel, and the Cooper Institute for Aerobics Research.

In his eating, Dr. Cooper is as fastidious as he is in his commitment to a healthy exercise regimen. His breakfast is the same every day: a grapefruit; a bran muffin; skim milk; and a cocktail of vitamin C, vitamin E, and beta carotene. Lunch is also the same each day: a cup of soup, salt-free crackers, and unsweetened iced tea. Dinner is slightly more gluttonous: fish or chicken (but never red meat) and vegetables like brussels sprouts, turnip greens, spinach, or cabbage.

Ah, but at night, Dr. Cooper really lets his hair down. Five nights a week he treats himself to a glass of skim milk and a few chocolate chip cookies.

wagon wheels

FREDA NADEAU   WARWICK, RHODE ISLAND

1¾ cups flour
1 teaspoon cinnamon
Dash of salt
¾ cup butter
⅔ cup packed brown sugar

1 egg
1 teaspoon vanilla extract
1 cup mini chocolate chips
¼ cup finely crushed chocolate
  wafers

Sift together the flour, cinnamon, and salt. Set aside.

Beat together the butter and brown sugar. Add egg and vanilla. Stir in flour mixture and chocolate chips. Batter will be very sticky.

Grease hands and countertop and shape batter into a 12-inch log. Roll log in crushed wafers, coating evenly. Wrap in plastic wrap and refrigerate overnight.

Preheat oven to 350°F.

Cut batter roll into ¼-inch to ½-inch slices. Place slices onto greased cookie sheets. Bake for 10 to 12 minutes.

yield: approximately 3 dozen cookies

The Sacred Chow, a health food store in Lower Manhattan, is the epitome of nutritional correctness. All the food is prepared without using refined sugar, white flour, or any animal products. A flavorful tart at the Sacred Chow contains soy and fennel sausage, fresh tomatoes, and garlic in a tender spelt and barley pastry. The lemon-caramel custard contains tofu and tapioca, and the salads are made with seaweed and couscous.

And, yes, the menu at the Sacred Chow does not ignore the traditional. There are chocolate chip cookies, with a strong taste of mint.

lunchbox favorite cookies

FLORENCE BROOKS   PETERSBURG, VIRGINIA

2½ cups flour	½ cup sugar
1 teaspoon baking soda	1¼ cups packed brown sugar
1 teaspoon baking powder	1 teaspoon vanilla extract
Dash of salt	2 eggs
1 cup shortening	1 cup chocolate chips
1½ cups peanut butter	1 cup blackberry preserves

Preheat oven to 350°F.

Sift together the flour, baking soda, baking powder, and salt. Set aside.

Beat together the shortening, peanut butter, sugar, brown sugar, vanilla, and eggs. Stir in flour mixture and chocolate chips.

Form batter into balls and place 1½ inches apart on greased cookie sheets. Press thumb into center of each cookie, forming a small crater. Spoon ½ teaspoon blackberry preserves into each crater. Make sure sides of crater form a complete wall to keep preserves from leaking out. Bake for 10 to 13 minutes.

yield: approximately 7 dozen cookies

rocky road cookie cakes

FAY KEDDINGTON   OGDEN, UTAH

2 cups flour
1 teaspoon baking powder
½ teaspoon baking soda
2 cups packed brown sugar
½ cup shortening
1 cup milk
3 eggs

1½ teaspoons vanilla extract
1 teaspoon almond extract
1 cup sliced almonds
1 cup mini marshmallows
½ cup semi-sweet chocolate chips
½ cup milk chocolate chips

Preheat oven to 350°F.

Sift together the flour, baking powder, baking soda, and brown sugar. Stir in shortening and mix well. Batter will be dry and crumbly. Set aside 1 cup of mixture.

Add milk, eggs, vanilla, almond extract, sliced almonds, marshmallows, semi-sweet chocolate chips, and milk chocolate chips to remaining mixture.

Pour batter into a greased 9 × 13-inch pan. Sprinkle reserved cup of flour mixture evenly over top. Bake for 40 to 45 minutes. Remove from oven and let cool. Cut into 1½-inch squares.

yield: approximately 4 dozen cookies

good-time cookies

EVELYN ISRAEL   BELLEVUE, WASHINGTON

1½ cups flaked coconut
3 cups flour
1 teaspoon baking soda
Dash of salt
1 cup sugar

1 cup shortening or margarine
1 egg
3 tablespoons rum
1 teaspoon vanilla extract
¾ cup chocolate chips

Preheat oven to 375°F.

Place coconut on a tray and bake for 8 to 10 minutes, stirring once or twice during baking. Remove from oven and set aside.

Sift together the flour, baking soda, and salt. Set aside.

Mix together the sugar, shortening, and egg. Stir in flour mixture, toasted coconut, rum, vanilla, and chocolate chips.

Drop by teaspoonfuls onto greased cookie sheets. Bake for 8 to 10 minutes.

yield: approximately 4½ dozen cookies

An extensive study was conducted to determine how food-buying practices of consumers in the United States have changed with the introduction of nutritional labels—showing fat, caloric, and nutritional content—on all packaged foods sold here.

It was found that during the six-month period starting three months before the labels were introduced and going to three months after, consumption of chocolate chip cookies increased by 10 percent.

In January 1996, when besieged First Lady Hillary Rodham Clinton arrived at the Borders Books store in Ann Arbor, Michigan, during her tour to promote her book It Takes a Village: And Other Lessons Children Teach Us, leaders of the Ann Arbor Hillary Rodham Clinton Fan Club were there to show their support. They handed out chocolate chip cookies made from Ms. Clinton's well-publicized personal recipe.

bob's butterscotch treats
ELEEN YOUNG   TEMPE, ARIZONA

1 cup sugar
½ cup margarine
1 cup flaked coconut
2 eggs
1½ cups flour

2 teaspoons baking powder
1 teaspoon baking soda
½ teaspoon salt
1 cup chocolate chips
¾ cup butterscotch syrup

Preheat oven to 375°F.

Beat sugar and margarine until creamy. Stir in coconut and eggs, mixing well. Add flour, baking powder, baking soda, and salt. Stir in chocolate chips.

Divide batter in half. Using dampened hands, press half of the batter into a greased 9 × 13-inch pan. Pour butterscotch syrup evenly over top. Again using dampened hands, pat remaining half of batter evenly over butterscotch syrup.

Bake for 22 to 25 minutes. Remove from oven and let cool. Cut into 1½-inch squares.

yield: approximately 4 dozen cookies

The Portland Wine and Cheese Shop is a gourmet sandwich establishment with an intriguing selection of breads, spreads, and fillings in the revitalized, ultra-trendy Old Port section of that seacoast city in Maine. What does it offer to its knowledgeable patrons?

How about sweet potato leek soup; roast beef on Canadian sourdough bread with horseradish sauce; dilled tuna on fresh homemade bread; and, for dessert, chocolate chip cookies that the regular customers enjoy unfailingly at the end of every meal.

double delights

MALCOLM GOODMAN   SAN JOSE, CALIFORNIA

1½ cups flour
½ cup unsweetened cocoa
    powder
1 teaspoon baking soda
½ teaspoon salt
¾ cup margarine or butter
2 eggs
1 cup sugar

½ cup brown sugar
1½ teaspoons vanilla extract
1 tablespoon chocolate syrup
¾ cup chopped walnuts
¾ cup chocolate chips
Vanilla Creme Filling (recipe
    follows)

Preheat oven to 350°F.

Sift together the flour, cocoa powder, baking soda, and salt. Set aside.

Beat together the margarine, eggs, sugar, brown sugar, vanilla, and chocolate syrup. Stir in flour mixture. Add walnuts and chocolate chips. Batter will be soft.

Drop by teaspoonfuls 2 inches apart onto greased cookie sheets. Bake 10 to 12 minutes. Remove from oven and let cool.

Spread Vanilla Creme Filling on top of half of the cookies and then cover filling with remaining cookies.

yield: approximately 2 dozen cookies

VANILLA CREME FILLING

2½ cups confectioners' sugar
3 tablespoons vanilla extract

½ cup unsalted margarine or
butter, softened

Mix together the confectioners' sugar, vanilla, and butter until creamy.

Who should know better what is good for you than the head of the Bellevue Hospital Center in New York City? The office of Pamela S. Brier, executive director of the medical center, has numerous bowls of M&M's placed about and a plate of chocolate chip cookies on the conference table.

Why does she spend nearly $1,000 of her own money each year for these treats? "It makes people comfortable," Ms. Brier explained. "When people are comfortable they say what they mean and they get things done."

Just think what a plate of chocolate chip cookies in every office in America would do for increasing national productivity.

yum yums

GILDA ARSENAULT   PORTLAND, MAINE

2 cups flour
1 teaspoon baking powder
½ cup peanut butter
¼ cup butter, softened
2 eggs

½ cup honey
½ cup milk or buttermilk
1½ cups chopped dried apples,
    apricots, peaches, and raisins
1 cup chocolate chips

Preheat oven to 350°F.

Sift together the flour and baking powder. Set aside.

Beat together the peanut butter and butter. Add eggs and honey. Add flour mixture and milk, alternately. Stir in dried fruits and chocolate chips.

Drop by teaspoonfuls onto greased cookie sheets. Bake for 10 to 12 minutes.

yield: *approximately 5½ dozen cookies*

The Iron Curtain fell, Communism disappeared, and Western capitalism arrived.

The throngs of American and other Western business people who have flocked to Czechoslovakia since the end of the Cold War to establish capitalistic ventures has resulted in its own boom of businesses to serve these foreigners. Indeed, at Ubiquity, an enormous disco—as big as a football field or two—in the capital city of Prague, where the music is far louder than any sounds of combat during the Cold War, the language heard almost exclusively is English with very little Czech. And, not surprising, the most popular foods served at Ubiquity are Mexican dishes, brownies, and chocolate chip cookies, all of which would be exotic delicacies for the native residents of the city.

chocolate malt chews

HELENE KIRKPATRICK   MIDWEST CITY, OKLAHOMA

2 egg whites
¼ teaspoon salt
½ cup sugar
½ teaspoon vinegar
1 teaspoon vanilla extract

¼ cup malted milk powder
1 cup milk chocolate, melted
½ cup chopped walnuts
½ cup chocolate chips

Preheat oven to 350°F.

Beat egg whites and salt until foamy. Gradually add sugar until stiff peaks form. Beat in vinegar and vanilla. Stir in malted milk powder. Add melted chocolate, walnuts, and chocolate chips, mixing well.

Drop by teaspoonfuls onto greased cookie sheets. Bake for 9 to 11 minutes. Remove from oven and then remove cookies from cookie sheets while still warm, using a slightly wet spatula.

yield: approximately 3 dozen cookies

date drops

JACQUELINE JACOBSEN   MINNEAPOLIS, MINNESOTA

½ cup chopped sugar-coated
   dates
¼ cup orange juice
2 cups flour
½ teaspoon baking soda
¼ teaspoon baking powder
Dash of salt

½ cup margarine
¾ cup sugar
¼ cup packed brown sugar
2 eggs
1½ teaspoons vanilla extract
1 cup chocolate chips

Preheat oven to 375°F.

Place dates and orange juice in a small heavy saucepan and bring to a boil. Boil, stirring, for 1 to 2 minutes. Remove from heat and set aside to cool.

Sift together the flour, baking soda, baking powder, and salt. Set aside.

Cream together the margarine, sugar, and brown sugar. Stir in eggs and vanilla. Stir in flour mixture. Mix in date mixture and chocolate chips. Batter will be very sticky.

Drop by teaspoonfuls onto greased cookie sheets. Bake for 9 to 11 minutes.

yield: approximately 6 dozen cookies

orange slice squares

HOPE FRANCIS   METAIRIE, LOUISIANA

1 cup margarine
½ cup sugar
½ cup packed brown sugar
2 eggs
1 tablespoon orange extract

2 cups flour
¼ teaspoon salt
1½ cups chopped orange-
    flavored fruit slice candies
1 cup chocolate chips

Preheat oven to 350°F.

Cream together the margarine, sugar, and brown sugar. Add eggs, orange extract, flour, salt, orange candies, and chocolate chips. Mix well.

Spread batter into a greased 8-inch-square pan. Pat down evenly with slightly dampened hands. Bake for 40 minutes. Remove from oven and let cool. Cut into 1½-inch squares.

yield: approximately 2 dozen cookies

Rejoice! Chocolate has entered the computer age. There is a Godiva On-line World Wide Web site:

http://www.godiva.com.

The Victorian Hudson River village of Cold Spring, New York, is a delightful destination for visitors who enjoy beautiful scenery, browsing for antiques, and shopping in boutiques, while going back in time to the small-town serenity of years ago.

At the Pig Hill Inn on Main Street, guests enjoy a breakfast composed of a heavenly light egg soufflé roll stuffed with spinach, mushrooms, and cream cheese; a basket of buttery biscuits; and a parfait dish filled with berries and heavy cream.

The antiques that furnish this charming stopover are also for sale. And in the afternoon, one of them increases in value. A plate of homemade chocolate chip cookies for everyone to enjoy is placed on an American farm table in the lobby. You can purchase this antique table for just $1,750, with the cookies included at no additional cost.

banana scotchers

JILL NEWTON   MILWAUKEE, WISCONSIN

2 eggs
½ cup plain yogurt
½ cup buttermilk
½ cup margarine, melted
2 cups flour
2 packages (3.4 ounces) instant
   banana cream pudding mix

1 tablespoon crème de banana
   liqueur
¾ cup butterscotch chips
¾ cup milk chocolate chips

Preheat oven to 350°F.

Stir eggs into yogurt and buttermilk. Add margarine, flour, and banana cream pudding mix. Stir in crème de banana liqueur, butterscotch chips, and chocolate chips. Batter will be sticky.

Drop by teaspoonfuls onto greased cookie sheets. Bake for 11 to 13 minutes, until cookies are brown around the bottom. Remove from oven and then remove cookies from cookie sheets while still warm.

yield: approximately 6 dozen cookies

What does a professional television viewer eat while doing his job? Jeff Jarvis, a critic for TV Guide who watches television about sixty hours a week, indulges in Coca-Cola, Cinnamon Graham Snacks, and Snackwell's Bite-Size Chocolate Chip Cookies.

yes! potato chips

MATTY MACDONALD   HALLANDALE, FLORIDA

1½ cups flour
¾ cup uncooked quick rolled oats
1 egg
1 teaspoon vanilla extract
½ teaspoon cream of tartar
½ cup margarine

½ cup vegetable oil
½ cup sugar
½ cup packed brown sugar
¾ cup chocolate chips
2½ cups thick-cut potato chips

Preheat oven to 350°F.

Mix together well the flour, oats, egg, vanilla, cream of tartar, margarine, oil, sugar, and brown sugar. Stir in chocolate chips and potato chips.

Drop by teaspoonfuls onto greased cookie sheets. Bake for 10 to 12 minutes.

yield: approximately 6 dozen cookies

Being President of the United States is not an easy job. There are heavy pressures and conflicts—regardless of how successful you are, how high your public approval ratings are, and how many of your legislative programs get passed into law.

Every President should be able to relax and enjoy those comforts of childhood, those things that bring back memories of when life was less complicated and less stressful. But President Bill Clinton cannot really enjoy the ultimate in comfort, fond memories, and happiness because he is allergic to chocolate and cannot eat chocolate chip cookies.

MGM Grand Air was a luxury airline that pampered its passengers flying between New York City and Los Angeles with DC-8s that carried only 71 passengers in a plane that normally seats 189. They were seated in spacious, living room–like areas; had a choice of three different movies; and got their baggage upon arrival in no more than seven minutes. All passengers received caviar, Champagne, and a lavish seven-course meal prepared by a chef right on board the plane, but the final extravagant amenity enjoyed by passengers was the package of chocolate chip cookies they received at the end of the flight.

peppermint chips

LEONARD HATHAWAY   FORT WAYNE, INDIANA

2½ cups flour
1 teaspoon baking soda
½ teaspoon salt
1 cup butter, softened
¾ cup sugar
¾ cup packed brown sugar

2 eggs
2 tablespoons chocolate mint
    liqueur
2 cups chocolate chips
1 cup coarsely chopped hard
    peppermint candies

Preheat oven to 375°F.

Sift together the flour, baking soda, and salt. Set aside.

Beat together the butter, sugar, and brown sugar. Add eggs and beat well. Stir in flour mixture, chocolate liqueur, chocolate chips, and peppermint candies.

Drop by teaspoonfuls 2 inches apart onto greased cookie sheets. Bake for 8 to 10 minutes.

yield: approximately 7 dozen cookies

Anza-Borrego Desert State Park in Southern California east of San Diego is the largest desert state park in the United States and the largest state park in all of California. The park offers a fascinating and very diverse desert experience, including vast empty expanses of natural beauty, unobstructed vistas of a big sky, an abundance of wildflowers in season, mountains and valleys, creosote bushes and cacti, early settlements of Cahuilla Indians, palm trees, wild bighorn sheep, still-visible ruts from stagecoach wheels, and even waterfalls and a nearby luxury resort.

La Casa del Zorro is just outside Borrego Springs, a small town surrounded by Anza-Borrego Desert State Park. The resort began in 1937 as a small ranchero and has grown now to be a truly lavish oasis with ninety-seven bedrooms (some in separate houses with their own swimming pools), three heated pools, a spa, a health club, and a conference center. The fireplaces in the rooms are cleaned and set up every day, guests wrap themselves in plush towels and robes, and the restaurant serves an eclectic menu with southwestern accents. But there is even more in this outpost of luxury. Guests can order freshly baked chocolate chip cookies and milk from room service.

mom's best

NINA LAWRENCE   YORK, PENNSYLVANIA

1 cup flour
½ teaspoon baking soda
Dash of salt
½ cup margarine or butter
½ cup sugar
½ cup brown sugar
1 egg

2 tablespoons milk
½ teaspoon vanilla extract
1 cup low-fat granola with
    raisins
1 cup chopped dates
1 cup chocolate chips

Preheat oven to 350°F.

Sift together the flour, baking soda, and salt. Set aside.

Mix together the margarine, sugar, and brown sugar. Add in egg, milk, and vanilla. Stir in flour mixture, granola, dates, and chocolate chips.

Drop by teaspoonfuls onto greased cookie sheets. Bake for 10 to 12 minutes. Remove cookies from cookie sheets while still slightly warm.

yield: approximately 4 dozen cookies

When President's Choice cookies were introduced in 1984, the company wanted an instant success in the marketplace. What kind of cookie did it choose for its initial offering? Decadent Chocolate Chip Cookies was the first variety sold, and it got the new brand of cookies off to a running start.

Bill Rogers, owner of the Red Barn boarding and training stables in Old Brookville, New York, has good reason to call the Guinness Book of World Records. The Red Barn is home to Mike, whom Mr. Rogers believes might be the largest horse in the world. Mike weighs around 3,500 pounds and stands 19½ hands—that is 6 feet, 6 inches, just to his shoulders.

Mike's daily diet is a bale and a half of hay, 20 pounds of grain, and 40 to 50 gallons of water. He also likes Halls cough drops—extra strength—as well as pizza and chocolate chip cookies.

coffee noodle doodles

SARAH CLAYTON   HONOLULU, HAWAII

1 cup margarine, softened
3 tablespoons instant coffee
    powder
¼ teaspoon salt
1 teaspoon almond extract

½ teaspoon vanilla extract
1 cup sugar
2 cups flour
2 cups mini chocolate chips
1½ cups chow mein noodles

Preheat oven to 375°F.

Cream together the margarine, coffee powder, salt, almond extract, and vanilla. Add sugar, mixing together well. Stir in flour, mixing well. Add chocolate chips and noodles.

Press batter into a 9 × 13-inch pan. Bake for 20 minutes. Remove from oven and let cool. Cut into 1½-inch squares.

yield: *approximately 4 dozen cookies*

Eric Lewin Altschuler, a physicist and mathematician, is the author of Bachanalia: The Essential Listener's Guide to Bach's Well-Tempered Clavier, *a guide to the great composer's most famous preludes and fugues. According to Mr. Altschuler's analyses and explanations, Bach's fugues can be compared to football plays, baseball teams, baseball players, circuses, children's games, screenplays, horror movies, meat and potatoes, candy bars, and chocolate chip cookies.*

And you thought it was just good music.

peanut butter double munchies

FLORENCE COFFEY   WEBSTER, NEW YORK

½ cup shortening
½ cup sugar
½ cup packed brown sugar
¾ cup chunky peanut butter
2 egg whites, beaten until foamy
1 teaspoon vanilla extract

1½ cups flour
1 teaspoon baking powder
1 cup peanuts
½ cup Grape Nuts cereal
1 cup chocolate chips

Preheat oven to 350°F.

Cream together the shortening, sugar, brown sugar, and peanut butter. Beat in egg whites and vanilla. Stir in flour and baking powder. Mix in peanuts, Grape Nuts cereal, and chocolate chips.

Drop by teaspoonfuls onto greased cookie sheets. Bake for 8 to 10 minutes.

yield: *approximately 5 dozen cookies*

The Kitchen Kabaret, a restaurant and gourmet food store on Long Island, east of New York City, offers a basket of "New York Street Food." Included in the collection are pieces of white and dark chocolate studded with M&M's; an egg cream in a bottle; peanut butter crunch; watermelon- and fancy-fruit-flavored popcorn; exotic jelly beans; cashew brittle; and last, but certainly not least, chocolate chip cookies.

fancy pants caramel-wiches

SONYA VELA   CORPUS CHRISTI, TEXAS

1 cup shortening
¾ cup sugar
¾ cup packed brown sugar
1½ teaspoons vanilla extract
2 eggs
2¼ cups flour
1 teaspoon baking soda
½ teaspoon salt

2 cups chocolate chips
1 cup chopped pecans
1 package (14 ounces) vanilla
  caramels
2 tablespoons water
14 ounces chocolate
¼ cup margarine

Preheat oven to 375°F.

Beat together the shortening, sugar, brown sugar, vanilla, and eggs. Stir in flour, baking soda, and salt, mixing together well. Add chocolate chips and pecans.

Drop by teaspoonfuls 1½ inches apart onto greased cookie sheets. Bake for 8 to 10 minutes. Remove cookies from cookie sheets and set aside to cool.

Place caramels and water in a heavy saucepan over low heat, stirring occasionally, until caramels have melted and mixed completely with water. Remove from heat and let cool slightly.

Using a small ladle, pour melted caramel onto the bottom of a cookie, then cover with another cookie, forming a sandwich. Until caramel filling sets, top cookie may slide off and need to be pushed back into position. Caramel may harden as cookie sandwiches are made. Reheat gently to regain desired consistency.

Combine chocolate and margarine in a heavy saucepan and heat gently over hot water until chocolate and margarine melt. Stir until smooth. Dip a quarter of each sandwich cookie into melted chocolate and place on wax paper to dry.

yield: approximately 3 dozen sandwich cookies

During the eight-day Passover holiday there are severe restrictions on the foods that observant Jews may eat, based on the ingredients and the way they are prepared. With advances in food technology, however, more and more foods that were previously forbidden have been reformulated and are now certified "Kosher for Passover." The Manischewitz Company, based in Jersey City, New Jersey, and one of the largest producers of food for Passover, is experimenting to produce Passover bagels, quiche, and chocolate chip cookies.

lime sophisticates

LEAH BUTLER   LEXINGTON, KENTUCKY

2 cups flour
1 teaspoon baking powder
½ teaspoon baking soda
Dash of salt
¼ teaspoon cinnamon
¾ cup butter, softened

1 cup sugar
2 tablespoons fresh lime zest
¼ cup fresh lime juice
1 cup semi-sweet chocolate chips
½ cup sugar mixed with ½
    teaspoon cinnamon

Preheat oven to 350°F.

Sift together the flour, baking powder, baking soda, salt, and cinnamon. Set aside.

Beat together the butter and sugar until light and fluffy. Add in lime zest and lime juice. Stir in flour mixture a little at a time. Mix in chocolate chips. Roll into small balls and then coat with cinnamon sugar.

Place balls 1 inch apart on greased cookie sheets. Bake for 13 to 15 minutes.

yield: approximately 4 dozen cookies

b&w's

JULIA PITTS   SHERWOOD, ARKANSAS

1½ cups flour
½ teaspoon baking soda
½ teaspoon baking powder
Dash of salt
¼ cup unsweetened cocoa
    powder
½ cup butter or margarine,
    melted

1 cup brown sugar
1 egg
½ cup buttermilk
1 tablespoon strong coffee
½ cup chopped pecans
1 cup white chocolate chips

Preheat oven to 375°F.

Sift together the flour, baking soda, baking powder, and salt. Set aside.

Mix cocoa powder into melted butter. Add brown sugar, egg, buttermilk, and coffee. Stir well. Stir in flour mixture. Add pecans and chocolate chips.

Drop by teaspoonfuls 2 inches apart onto greased cookie sheets. Bake for 10 to 12 minutes.

yield: approximately 4½ dozen cookies

mint meringues

LESLIE TOWNSEND   LAS VEGAS, NEVADA

4 egg whites
1⅓ cups sugar
½ teaspoon salt

1 teaspoon peppermint extract
2 cups mint chocolate chips

Preheat oven to 350°F.

Beat egg whites until stiff. Fold in sugar and salt. Gently fold in peppermint extract and chocolate chips.

Drop by teaspoonfuls close together onto cookie sheets that have been covered with aluminum foil. Place cookie sheets in preheated oven, turn off oven, and leave oven door closed for 8 hours.

yield: approximately 6 dozen cookies

Aqua, a much-acclaimed, extravagant seafood restaurant in San Francisco's business district, offers diners a selection of innovative foods not usually found on the menus of other restaurants. For example, you can order sautéed foie gras with apples, Calvados along with a Sauternes jelly, Dungeness crab cakes with a saffron vinaigrette containing slivers of strong raw garlic, breaded and pounded abalone served over black olive fettuccine with added pine nuts and sweet peppers, and sea scallops with couscous sweetened with dried fruit.

But if you want to get back to your roots and your comforting thoughts of childhood, Aqua does have just the right desserts after your ultra-trendy appetizers and entrées. You can conclude your dinner by sipping a root beer float through a chocolate straw and chewing on some delicious warm chocolate chip cookies.

Aqua certainly gives a sparkling combination of the ultra-trendy and the ultra-traditional.

twice-baked nuttiness

LIBBY SOMMERER   GRANDVIEW, MISSOURI

1½ cups chopped macadamia nuts
1 cup shortening
½ cup packed brown sugar
1 tablespoon instant coffee powder
½ teaspoon cinnamon
½ teaspoon salt

2 cups flour
3 eggs
1 tablespoon rum
1 cup sugar
1 cup flaked coconut
1 cup milk chocolate chips

Preheat oven to 325°F.

Spread chopped macadamia nuts in a single layer in a shallow pan and bake for 6 to 8 minutes. Remove from oven and set aside.

Beat together the shortening, brown sugar, coffee powder, cinnamon, and ¼ teaspoon of the salt, until light and fluffy. Add in flour and mix well. Batter will be crumbly.

Spread into a greased 9 × 13-inch pan. Bake for 20 minutes. Remove from oven and set aside to cool for 20 to 25 minutes.

Beat together the eggs, rum, sugar, and remaining ¼ teaspoon salt. Stir in macadamia nuts, coconut, and chocolate chips.

Spread evenly over cooled cookies in pan. Return pan to oven and continue baking at 325°F for 40 to 45 minutes. Remove from oven and loosen edges from sides of pan with a knife. Let cool, then cut into 1½-inch squares.

yield: approximately 4 dozen cookies

Since dogs are man's best friend, don't they deserve to have the best that humans have? Alpo Petfoods obviously thinks so, since the company has introduced Alpo Beef Chip Cookies, a crunchy treat for dogs that is baked, shaped, and packaged just like chocolate chip cookies. There is a limit, though, to anthropomorphism. The Alpo Beef Chip Cookies do not have any chocolate in them.

technicolor treats

MARCIA HAMMONDS   TUSCALOOSA, ALABAMA

1½ cups ground almonds
1¾ cups flour
1 cup sugar
¾ cup plus 2 tablespoons butter
   or margarine, melted

1 teaspoon vanilla extract
1 teaspoon almond extract
½ cup M&M's Mini Baking Bits
½ cup chocolate chips
Sugar

Preheat oven to 425°F.

Mix together the almonds, flour, and sugar. Pour in melted butter, vanilla, and almond extract. Add M&M's Mini Baking Bits and chocolate chips. Mix well.

Form into 1-inch balls. Place balls on greased cookie sheets and flatten with the bottom of a drinking glass that has been dipped into sugar. Bake for 8 to 10 minutes.

yield: approximately 4 dozen cookies

Traveling today can be a lot more exciting than just a visit to the Grand Canyon or the Eiffel Tower. You can float in a balloon over the California wine country, cruise to Antarctica on a Russian icebreaker, trek through the mountains of Nepal, be an ecotourist in Costa Rica, and make the rounds of lighthouses in New Zealand or the rose gardens of England. But the most tasteful trips of all are the organized tours of chocolate makers throughout Belgium.

cinnamon applesaucies

LYDIA SAAD   DEARBORN, MICHIGAN

1 cup whole wheat flour
1 cup flour
1 teaspoon baking soda
½ teaspoon baking powder
Dash of salt
1½ teaspoons cinnamon
½ cup shortening

½ cup sugar
½ cup brown sugar
1 egg
1 cup cinnamon applesauce
1 cup uncooked quick rolled oats
½ cup raisins
1 cup chocolate chips

Preheat oven to 375°F.

Sift together the whole wheat flour, flour, baking soda, baking powder, salt, and cinnamon. Set aside.

Beat together the shortening, sugar, brown sugar, egg, and applesauce. Stir in flour mixture, oats, raisins, and chocolate chips.

Drop by teaspoonfuls onto greased cookie sheets. Bake for 8 to 10 minutes.

yield: approximately 5 dozen cookies

campfire memories

LIZ EHRLICH   LINCOLN, NEBRASKA

1 cup margarine, softened
¼ cup sugar
¼ cup confectioners' sugar
1 teaspoon vanilla extract
2 cups flour

½ cup chopped walnuts
1 cup milk chocolate chips
1½ to 2 cups mini marshmallows
Confectioners' sugar

Preheat oven to 375°F.

Cream together the margarine, sugar, and confectioners' sugar. Add vanilla, flour, walnuts, and chocolate chips, mixing together well.

Roll into small balls and place onto greased cookie sheets. Press 3 or 4 marshmallows into top of each cookie, slightly flattening cookie. Bake for 9 to 11 minutes. Remove from oven and let cool for 5 minutes. Sprinkle confectioners' sugar over top of cookies.

yield: approximately 5 dozen cookies

mocha monsters

ADA MUNOZ   OXNARD, CALIFORNIA

2 cups flour
Dash of salt
½ cup shortening
½ cup margarine
¼ cup sugar
¾ cup packed brown sugar
1 tablespoon instant coffee
    dissolved in 1 teaspoon hot
    water

2 ounces unsweetened
    chocolate, melted and
    cooled
1 egg
1½ cups chocolate chips
½ cup confectioners' sugar

Preheat oven to 350°F.

Mix together the flour and salt. Set aside.

Beat together the shortening and margarine until soft. Add sugar and brown sugar and continue beating until fluffy. Stir in dissolved coffee, melted chocolate, and egg. Beat well. Stir in flour mixture and chocolate chips.

Roll batter into 2-inch balls and place on greased cookie sheets. Dip bottom of a glass into confectioners' sugar and slightly press on cookie balls to flatten. Bake for 10 to 12 minutes.

yield: *approximately 2 dozen cookies*

In the "HERS" column in The New York Times, *Deborah Gimelson, a writer who usually specializes in art but who wrote a book about the socio-cultural aspects of women and fitness, related her love affair with her personal trainer from her gym. The affair ended rather abruptly and unhappily when he dumped her, not surprisingly, since he had been cheating on her all along. To comfort herself after the breakup, Ms. Gimelson says she "Nursed my sense of abandonment with chocolate chip cookies."*

It's nice to know you always have a sympathetic friend.

broken oven chocolate lemon balls

STELLA GROTE NORWOOD, OHIO

1 cup finely crushed brown-
 edged wafer cookies
1½ cups confectioners' sugar
2 tablespoons unsweetened
 cocoa powder
½ cup ground hazelnuts

½ cup ground pecans
2 tablespoons light corn syrup
3 tablespoons orange juice
1 teaspoon lemon extract
¾ cup mini chocolate chips
Sugar

Combine cookies, confectioners' sugar, cocoa powder, hazelnuts, pecans, corn syrup, orange juice, lemon extract, and chocolate chips, mixing together well.

Roll cookies into walnut-sized balls and then coat with sugar. Batter will be very sticky. After rolling 1 or 2 cookie balls, coat palms of hands with sugar.

yield: approximately 3 dozen cookies

Different people have different ways of feeling secure, from a childhood blanket to direct, uncensored access to the Internet. For restaurant critic Eric Asimov, security can take the form of a charming and affordable little restaurant not too far from the Broadway theater district in Manhattan, or a package of chocolate chip cookies safely hidden away.

Oh, yes. His security restaurant is Topaz, a Thai restaurant just around the block from Carnegie Hall.

toasted almond rum raisin balls

SYLVIA HARRELL   WHITEHALL, OHIO

⅓ cup rum
⅓ cup uncooked quick rolled oats
⅔ cup golden raisins
⅔ cup slivered almonds
2 cups confectioners' sugar
¼ teaspoon ground nutmeg

¼ teaspoon cinnamon
⅓ cup margarine, melted and
   cooled
1 cup chocolate chips
Sugar

Mix together the rum, oats, and raisins and let soak for 2 hours.

Preheat oven to 350°F.

Place almonds in a single layer in a shallow pan and bake for 6 to 8 minutes, stirring once or twice, until lightly toasted. Remove from oven and set aside.

Add toasted almonds, confectioners' sugar, nutmeg, cinnamon, margarine, and chocolate chips to rum mixture. Batter will be soft.

Form into 1½-inch balls and roll in sugar. Let cookies stand for at least 24 hours before serving to bring out the flavor.

yield: approximately 3 dozen cookies

It seems that no matter where you go, you will always run into chocolate chip cookies.

Guests at the Millamolong Station, a working farm in New South Wales, Australia, who go out riding on the horse trails are treated to an elaborate picnic brought out by the farm staff in a four-wheel-drive vehicle. Picnic blankets are spread out on the riverbank, bottles of wine are put in the water to cool, and a wide variety of foods—even a quiche—are spread out. For dessert in the Australia outback, there is coffee and, fortunately, chocolate chip cookies.

cranberry flakers

PEGGY INGRAM   NEWARK, DELAWARE

1 cup flour
1 teaspoon baking powder
¼ teaspoon salt
⅓ cup butter, softened
1 cup sugar

1 egg
1 teaspoon vanilla extract
½ cup dried cranberries
1 cup chocolate chips
2 cups corn flakes cereal

Preheat oven to 375°F.

Sift together the flour, baking powder, and salt. Set aside.

Beat together the butter, sugar, egg, and vanilla. Stir in flour mixture, cranberries, chocolate chips, and corn flakes. Mix together well.

Drop by teaspoonfuls onto greased cookie sheets. Bake for 9 to 11 minutes.

yield: *approximately 4 dozen cookies*

Politicians like to show that they know everything about everything to instill confidence in the voters at election time. But many areas of government are sometimes too complicated or too esoteric for anyone but a few experts to understand. It is usually best, therefore, to stick with what you—and your constituents—know and understand. That approach appeared to be the philosophy of New Jersey Governor Jim Florio.

At a heavily covered media event for the ground-breaking of a $60-million transportation rail link in the northern part of the state, the governor, after leading reporters into a special rail car filled with refreshments set up for the day, declared, "There are few things I am an expert on: cheesecake, ice cream, pizza, and chocolate chip cookies."

ginger snips

VERNA OWENS   MT. PLEASANT, SOUTH CAROLINA

¾ cup margarine, softened
1½ cups sugar
1 egg
¼ cup molasses
2 cups flour

2 teaspoons baking soda
¼ teaspoon salt
1 teaspoon cinnamon
1 tablespoon ground ginger
1 cup chocolate chips

Preheat oven to 350°F.

Mix together well the margarine, 1 cup of the sugar, and egg. Stir in molasses, flour, baking soda, salt, cinnamon, and ginger. Add chocolate chips.

Roll batter into small balls and roll in the remaining ½ cup of the sugar. Place 2 inches apart on greased cookie sheets. Bake 1 cookie sheet at a time on center rack of oven for 11 to 13 minutes.

yield: approximately 4½ dozen cookies

A visit to New York City can be a fascinating experience, and a chance to discover many new and exciting things. In the movie Home Alone 2: Lost in New York, the first thing Macaulay Culkin did when his family checked into the Plaza Hotel was head for the in-room refrigerator for candy and chocolate chip cookies. He probably wanted assurances that whatever strange and unexpected adventures you might have, at least there is one thing familiar you can count on.

crispies

TINA GILLISPIE   CHARLESTON, WEST VIRGINIA

½ cup butter, softened
½ cup sugar
½ cup packed brown sugar
1 teaspoon vanilla extract
1 egg
1 cup flour

1 teaspoon baking powder
Dash of salt
1 cup uncooked quick rolled oats
¾ cup flaked coconut
1 cup chocolate chips
1 cup crisp rice cereal

Preheat oven to 325°F.

Cream together the butter, sugar, and brown sugar. Beat in vanilla and egg. Stir in flour, baking powder, and salt. Mix in oats, coconut, and chocolate chips. Gently stir in crisp rice cereal.

Roll batter into small balls and place on greased cookie sheets. Bake for 15 to 20 minutes.

yield: *approximately 5 dozen cookies*

Who would have thought that chocolate chip cookies could be part of an educational lesson on the environment? William R. Einsig, a curriculum development specialist in the West Shore School District in suburban Harrisburg, Pennsylvania, that's who.

Einsig has designed a classroom exercise that shows the possible environmental damage that can be caused when extracting minerals from the earth. Chocolate chip cookies are distributed to students along with toothpicks. The task is to remove the chocolate chips from the cookies with the toothpicks—mine them, if you will—and then repair the damage caused to the cookies by the removal process, an obvious impossibility.

The objective of Mr. Einsig's demonstration is to create an awareness of the changes in the environment that are caused by various human activities.

chocolate no-bake oat squares

TERRY RAY   CHATTANOOGA, TENNESSEE

2 cups sugar
½ cup margarine
½ cup milk
1 cup peanut butter
2 teaspoons maple flavoring
1 teaspoon vanilla extract

3 cups uncooked quick rolled
oats
1½ cups regular-size chocolate
chips
1 cup mini chocolate chips

Heat sugar, margarine, and milk in a heavy saucepan, stirring until sugar dissolves. Boil for 2 minutes. Add peanut butter, maple flavoring, and vanilla.

Remove from heat and add oats and regular-size chocolate chips. Stir well, until chocolate chips have melted completely.

Using dampened hands, spread cookie dough into a 10 × 15-inch rectangle on wax paper. Let cool slightly and then press mini chocolate chips evenly into top of dough. Cut into 1½-inch squares.

yield: approximately 6 dozen cookies

During the severe Mississippi River flooding during the summer of 1993, many women worked long hours alongside men shoring up the levees, filling sandbags, and building flood walls as well as doing the laundry for the people working day after day to control the rising waters.

One of the women's most welcome contributions was the hundreds and hundreds of batches of chocolate chip cookies that they baked for everyone working along the flooding riverbanks.

It is customary for the mayors of the two cities whose teams are competing in the National Football League Super Bowl to have a wager, each offering a well-known local product for the bet.

When the Buffalo Bills played the Washington Redskins in Super Bowl XXVI in 1992, the mayor of Buffalo, not surprisingly, put up 100 Buffalo wings, the hot and spicy deep-fat-fried chicken wings. For Mayor Sharon Pratt Kelly of Washington, D.C., this tradition caused a slight problem. The main local product of the nation's capital is government, and it did not seem appropriate to offer 100 feet of red tape, a congressional fillibuster, or a complete set of IRS forms. She finally settled on a case of chocolate chip cookies from a program that had inner city youths manufacturing and distributing the cookies.

Since the Redskins beat the Bills 37 to 24, Mayor Pratt got to enjoy the Buffalo wings—with Washington's chocolate chip cookies for dessert.

absolute almond

THELMA WHITE   CHEYENNE, WYOMING

1 cup chopped almonds
¾ cup butter, softened
½ cup sugar
1 egg

2 teaspoons amaretto liqueur
1 teaspoon almond extract
2 cups flour
1 cup chocolate chips

Preheat oven to 350°F.

Place chopped almonds in a single layer in a shallow pan and bake for 6 to 8 minutes, stirring once or twice, until lightly toasted. Remove from oven and set aside.

Increase oven temperature to 375°F.

Cream together the butter and sugar. Add in egg, amaretto liqueur, and almond extract. Stir in flour and mix well. Stir in toasted almonds and chocolate chips.

Drop by teaspoonfuls 1 inch apart onto greased cookie sheets. Bake for 8 to 10 minutes.

yield: approximately 4½ dozen cookies

toasted coconut crispies

ROSEMARIE DaSILVA   DANBURY, CONNECTICUT

1 cup flaked coconut
1 cup flour
1 teaspoon baking soda
Dash of salt
½ cup margarine or butter

¾ cup sugar
1 teaspoon vanilla extract
1 egg
1 cup chocolate chips

Preheat oven to 375°F.

Spread coconut in a shallow pan and bake, stirring often, for 8 to 10 minutes, until golden. Remove from oven and set aside.

Sift together the flour, baking soda, and salt. Set aside.

Beat together the margarine, sugar, vanilla, and egg. Stir in flour mixture. Add chocolate chips and toasted coconut. Mix together well.

Drop by teaspoonfuls onto greased cookie sheets. Bake for 10 to 12 minutes.

yield: *approximately 6 dozen cookies*

In the movie Trading Mom, Sissy Spacek plays a much-harried single mother with three small children. Since she demands some help from them, like cleaning up their rooms, the three children enlist the help of a magical neighbor who gives them a choice of new moms at the Mommy Market, sort of a mall where replacement mothers are displayed.

The possible choices included: a wealthy Frenchwoman with a maid, a cook, and the longest cigarette holder in the world; an outdoorswoman who enjoys camping out in the rain; and a Russian clown. None of them appealed to the children. The obvious choice for Harry, one of the young boys, was the mommy who had chocolate chip cookies stuck to her headband.

The population of Ocean Beach, a one-half-square-mile beach town on Fire Island in New York, goes from about 150 people in the winter to over 15,000 during the summer. The town must therefore be strict in its ordinances regarding noise, littering, and other public quality-of-life crimes. Like eating in public.

Back in 1977, Ocean Beach got international attention when one young man was charged with eating a chocolate chip cookie in public while his friend was similarly cited for eating a crumb cake. Happily for these two hardened criminals, the charges of eating in public were dropped after the village prosecutor, joining with defense attorneys, noted that the police were enforcing the anti-eating laws in an inconsistent manner. Cookie eaters were being issued summonses but ice-cream-cone lickers were getting away completely free.

index